INNER VOYAGER

Yaffa Baran
Inner Voyager

All rights reserved
Copyright © 2023 by **Yaffa Baran**

No part of this publication may be reproduced, distributed, or transmitted in any form
or by any means, including photocopying, recording, or other electronic or mechanical
methods, without the prior written permission of the publisher, except in the case of
brief quotations embodied in critical reviews and certain other noncommercial uses
permitted by copyright law.

Published by BooxAi
ISBN:978-965-578-657-6

INNER VOYAGER

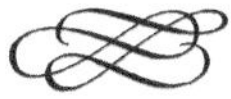

YAFFA BARAN

I dedicate this book in the memory of my loving mother and to all the mothers who have endured the pain of losing their children to the ravages of war, terror, tyranny, and savagery.

I am grateful to the Creator for choosing me as a vessel to convey His glory and greatness through my poetry. I extend my heartfelt thanks to my family for believing in me—my brother for his unwavering support. My daughter played an essential role in designing the book's cover, and my son's suggestions have been invaluable. I owe a debt of gratitude to my dear friend Lida, who encouraged me to publish this collection, allowing my voice to be shared. Lastly, I extend my deepest thanks to my remarkable teacher, Dr. Michael Laitman (Rav), whose tireless efforts have bestowed me with wisdom, fostering a sense of connection and unity through love. He has guided me on my journey of transformation into the collective soul of Adam HaRishon(First Man).

CONTENTS

INTRODUCTION

Rather than recounting the details of my personal journey, I extend a heartfelt invitation for you to delve deep into the profound desires that form the foundation of my poetry. This is an invitation to enter the sacred inner chamber of my words, a place where rebellion, agony, and transformation reside. As you navigate through the rooms of this poetic dwelling, you'll uncover a part of yourself that may have long been forgotten —a reflection in the verses that transcends mere words.

In every layer of emotion, you might catch glimpses of your own soul mirrored in my verses, as if you were living my experiences. This shared connection between poet and reader opens a gateway to self-discovery and a deeper understanding of your inner yearnings, offering a chance to feel and experience your true self and your purpose through the prism of my words.

My ultimate aspiration is that this journey into my inner world touches the deepest recesses of your heart and soul, bringing forth the joy of rebirth. It doesn't matter what tumultuous paths you've tread or what bittersweet experiences life has offered, for each of these moments, be they bitter or sweet, weaves an integral thread in the rich tapestry of life.

I extend my love and gratitude to all of you; it is your presence that breathes life into my words. It is your willingness to accompany me on this journey through the labyrinth of human emotions, in all their raw and unfiltered forms, that fuels my creativity and drives my pen.

As you take this expedition through my verses, you may find yourself immersed in the raw essence of human existence, caught in the ebb and flow of love and pain, joy and sorrow, success and failure. Poetry is a vessel that transcends the boundaries of time and space, carrying us to places we've never been, allowing us to relive moments long past, and offering a glimpse of what the future may hold.

Each poem is a drop in the vast ocean of human experience, a testament to the myriad emotions and struggles that define our lives. Within these verses, you'll discover the resilience of the human spirit, the unbreakable bond of human connection, and the ever-evolving journey of self-discovery.

In the depths of these words, you might find solace for your own trials and tribulations, inspiration for your personal odyssey, and the strength to overcome whatever obstacles may come your way. This poetry is not just my story; it's a shared narrative of the human experience, a reflection of our collective dreams and desires.

In the darkest moments of despair, you'll find a glimmer of hope. In the embrace of pain, you'll discover the seed of resilience. And within the lines of my verses, you'll encounter the whispers of your own soul, calling out for exploration and understanding.

This poetic odyssey is an intimate dialogue between my heart and yours, an exchange of emotions and experiences that transcend the boundaries of language and culture. My words are a bridge, connecting us across the chasms of our individual lives, reminding us that we are never truly alone in our struggles and triumphs. We are with divine a loving force of bestowal.

So, as you embark on this journey through the vast landscape of my poetry, I invite you to immerse yourself fully in the emotions, the stories, and the dreams that unfurl before you. May you find solace, inspiration, and a profound connection with the human experience that unites us all, and may you emerge from this voyage with a renewed sense of purpose, a deeper understanding of your own desires, and a heart filled with the enduring love and compassion that binds us together.

TERRORISTS IN THE SHADOWS

The mother's sobbing rends humanity's core,

    Her broken heart, a curse, haunts Terrorists evermore.

Anger shatters the walls of cruel genocide,

Her bleeding sorrow eclipses the Sun's bright tide.

Her hatred, an iron arrow, pierces malevolent hearts.

Savage terrorist, your dark existence departs.

Heaven weeps for every breath, every life you've taken,

Even hell's gates shun your face, now forsaken.

Satan himself, your existence does shame,

The wrath of God upon you, an eternal flame.

2023

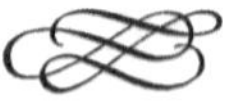

THE DEVOURING NIGHT

A foggy night, pregnant with sin, a place both distant and close to home,

Silence whispers the tale of forgotten tribes, a history concealed in the gloom,

Cricket chirp, spinning the story of the lost bride in the shadowy night,

Silence in tow, their whistling takes flight, enveloped in eerie fright.

Darkness, immersed in silence, calls upon the dubious wind,

A wicked chill drills through the bones, and icy cloak in this desolate place

Laughter muffles, a ghost in the uninhabited ruins, a specter of the past,

Bats squeak in the mirage of scorched wood, in time's echo, they're cast.

A glowing dream catcher fades as the wolf's moans intensify in the air's decay.

A pulsating heart, entangled with the Curse of the Ninth, in the night's eerie ballet.

The decomposed corpse screeches, trembling in the face of its fate,

Death devours the horror of the night, sealing its victims' bleak state.

Time freezes, movement halts, and images dissipate, yet spirit liberates,

In this chilling realm of the unknown, where the shadows dedicated their fate.

2 0 2 2

EGO'S DEFEAT

The bony hands of defeated ego knock upon your heart's door,
The claws of misery scratch at the threshold of your mind's core.

Evil inclination disguises itself, seeking refuge in your thoughts,

Yet you stand resolute, lifting the holy Shechina from the dust,

And you surrender to the unwavering power of LOVE.

2022

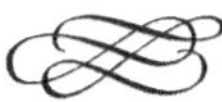

THE SANCTUARY OF GOD

I wandered through a winding alley of contemplation, seeking God's grace,

Numerous enchanting doors emerged, from ages past to present embrace,

Gently, I knocked on each door, where faint whispers beckoned,

Obediently, I ventured forth, harboring no trepidation.

Resolute in my quest to uncover the divine countenance's revelation.

Every realm's beauty seized my senses, an exquisite presence,

Enveloping me in the resonance of wisdom, chants, and self-discipline's essence.

I found myself entranced, ensnared by its beguiling allure,

Yet not wholly ensnared, my thoughts retained their tether, secure.

As if an unseen hand guided me through this interconnected realm,

I heeded the call, "Join me," like a sleepwalking in a dream's helm.

And extinguished the light behind an alluring "BB" door,

I embraced this magnificent abode, heart racing with anticipation evermore.

Discovering the Sanctuary of God, the Sanctuary of Love,

The Sanctuary of Friendship, the Sanctuary of Unity from below to above.

I felt His omnipotence, witnessed the splendor of the Lord's embrace,

As time passed, my yearnings underwent a transformation, a divine grace.

A longing to serve the Almighty welled up within me, a sacred flame,

Growing stronger, I pledged myself as His steadfast companion, to proclaim.

Continuing along this sacred path, without a backward glance, I tread,

Joyous, I closed my mortal eyes, and followed my inner vision, where it led.

Deeper I go, my being yearns to be the queen of your kingdom,

Toward the celestial realm, I journey, in a spiritual anthem.

In the sacred sanctuary, my soul finds its eternal home,

As I move closer to God, no matter where my feet may roam.

Note: BB(Beni Baruch)

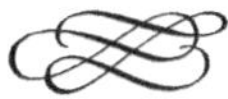

JOY IN ASHES

Trapped in the golden cage of ego's sway,

Chained with beastly desires, night and day.

Evil camouflages amid ruins of our thoughts,

Fear follows the dark shadow, as if it's never fought.

The rustic lock of Stoney's heart disintegrates,

Hope burns like a disfigured, melted candle at the gates.

Joy crumbles to ashes and conforms to dust's might,

As help shirks with a creepy face, and courage takes flight.

Only the observer remains detached from self-conceit,

In their gaze, the inner truth they seek to meet.

In this unending quest for wisdom and inner grace,

They find solace in the stillness of the observer's space.

THE MASTER'S REDEMPTION

Master of the universe, bestow your glory upon the shattered hearts

Awaken your people from the abyss of night's haunting fears, where darkness departs.

Proclaim your holiness to the ten lost tribes, we implore,

Set forth and liberate us from Egyptian slavery once more.

Rescue us from the inner turmoil, from self-destruction's snare,

For in your hands alone resides the key to salvation, locked gates,

Illuminate the darkness, reveal the evil inclination that does resides,

Within our very essence, let your light be our guide.

Purify us, that we may bask in your divine glory,

And let our souls sing of your eternal story.

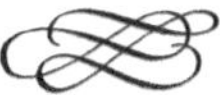

MY RAV

You are the thorn to my intellectual faculty's domain,

A fatherly love in a realm of distinct reality's terrain.

My Moses, pulling me from the depths of life's filthy pit,

My Noah, rescuing me from the city of sin's snare.

You are the key to the gate of liberation's door,

Challenging, extending my boundaries once more.

You whirl my thoughts like a tempest's vibrant creation,

With all my heart and might, I love you, no hesitations.

You light up my darkest nights, my beacon's guiding glow,

The flower of my heart, nurturing without ceasing, I know.

You are the melody to my ears, my Rav, my guide,

At a loss for words, my gratitude and aw coincide.

Your love and devotion envelop us with a gentle touch,

You are the father to whom my soul is forever bound, as such.

You are the Teacher to whom I humbly bow down,

In your wisdom, I find my purpose and my crown.

ART OF CONNECTION

Let us embrace the holy Schechina in our gathering with utmost care,

In the company of friends, we glimpse the Creator's glory, the darkness we bear.

Acknowledge both left and right forces, be brave and true,

The holy Schechina, ever present, will guide us through.

Sensitivity allows us to discern the Creator's radiant hand,

And recognize the lurking evil inclination that may stand.

Let us praise the good, wrestle with the bad,

As a united Ten, rise above in joy, ever expanding.

Hijack not friends' desires for selfish gain, we pledge,

As the Creator knocks, welcome with hearts that won't hedge.

In assembly, maintain the connection, don't let it wane,

And resist rigidity in perception for growth to be attained.

Walking the talk, even when our bodies may rebel,

Feel more, sense more, practice, our connection to fulfill.

In our unity, the Creator's presence, we will discern,

Fully awake and open-hearted, with gratitude in return.

Embrace each other's requests, be flexible despite inconvenience's cost,

Release the hold of Pharaoh, let self-love be lost.

Living the Kabbalist life with all our might,

For the Creator's tests upon us, day and night.

Kindness towards one another, giving space to each one's shine,

Nourish our environment, so no one thinks to resign,

Let's unite our spirits, grow stronger in our quest,

For in unity and love, we reveal the Lord's Glory, We'r truly blessed.

Note: The Shechina is G-d as G-d is dwelling within.

JOURNEY THROUGH THE HAZE

The past dissolves into the misty air,

Old memories swirl in a hazy dance, beyond compare,

As joyful songs fall silent, a somber trance.

I find myself reborn in an unfamiliar existence,

Every corner, foreign and intangible, a new distance.

It's a quiet chapter, one of stillness and numbness,

A peaceful interlude in the cold, dark, solitary expanse.

At the bottom, it's daunting, yet at the summit, comforting,

The new series of my life stretches on, a distant and misty journey, never-ending.

I must traverse it step by step, ascending the ladder,

Glimpsing at the veiled life, yearning for clarity, and what it might scatter.

In this harsh garment, I acquaint myself with the new me,

I must embrace the unique role I now portray, for all to see.

Colors, new and vibrant, paint over my life's canvas,

I must dance with the enigmatic creatures of the night, understand their ethos.

In this journey of discovery, I find my way home.

A transformation that shapes me, as I continue to roam.

THE DUEL WITHIN

What do I see, and what do I feel? Are we truly one?

Life grins, yet you linger in somber despair, undone.

As life bestows its radiance upon me, you remain cloaked in shadows,

The melodies of life serenade my senses, while specters of death haunt you, in endless rows.

Life's splendor unfurls, but horrors overshadow your perspective,

I bask in life's embrace, while you remain numb to its touch, I'd give your directive.

The gift of life I embrace, yet it clutches you with sorrow,

Love envelops me, while you open your heart to hatred alone, and it's hared to swallow.

Joy beckons to me, but agony reverberates in your ears,

Life appears flawless in my eyes, while you uncover its imperfections, causing tears.

Where gentle breezes soothe my soul, lightning strikes your fear,

The warmth of a safety blanket enfolds me, as winter beats you down, severely.

I receive a mother's nurturing care, while you sense a father's heartless.

Life is the very essence of existence, but your reality languishes in a void, heartless.

Why are we so disparate, you and I? Why?

Why do we feel estranged, like two souls inhabiting a single bod, under the sky?

Two facets of one countenance, love and hate, night and day,

Darkness and light, the tale of our existence we've long known.

In ceaseless conflict within, enduring as far back as memory extends,

Yet there persists a glimmer of hope that someday, in unity, we may become whole, as love transcends.

THE KINGDOM OF DARK THOUGHTS

You sit on a damp bench on a familiar night,

The Silence's rotten air is heavy, its repulsive smell, a wretched plight.

You feel possessed by the kingdom of dark thoughts,

Thoughts come like a tornado, spinning and destroying, tying you in knots.

Like a sharp blade slicing your being, though no physical contact made,

Trapping your true identity with a rustic chain to the unwanted demands that never fade.

Dragging you through the long, ugly alley of the forgotten people,

wrapping you with rough old ropes of intolerance,

Rising from the grave with its bony hands, it squeezes freedom out of you,

Its gloomy, smoky cloud covers your liberated mind, hiding love from view.

Its invisible curse travels far, casting ignorance and hatred.

Condemning compassion, unity, friendship, and love of humanity,
and all that's sacred.

It yells unrecognized, unwanted names while staring at you,

It's the covenant with you, the last life partnership that you despise,
and it's true.

Its prejudice, injustice, and wicked authority over you are sickening,

Raining dominance day and night, the torment it keeps brining.

But you know, deep in your heart, there's only one force governing
your existence,

But you know with all your might, there's only one loving force
shining upon you, in insistence.

It's the love of friends, love of humanity, the unity you hold dear,

The love of liberation, of oneness, wholeness and the Creator, clear.

2 0 2 2

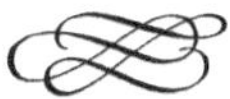

LOST IN DESPAIR

You sit there alone,

Holding your knees, gazing down in despair, on your own.

Fixated on the floor, as if a portal might open,

Or as if the entire world unfolds at that very point, your heart is broken.

As if time itself has frozen in your presence,

Lost, confused, disoriented, and disconnected, seeking transcendence.

Numb and burdened, half-frozen, you ponder:

Who am I? Where am I bound, you wonder?

Where is the purpose of this life?

How did I reach this place, and what's my role in this endless strife?

Why do I shiver in this cold embrace?

Where has the sun vanished without a trace?

When did clouds obscure reality's sight?

Shifting, as if you've entered another dimension, day into night.

Devoid of life's vibrancy, color, scent, or sound,

A world where even sights are absent, bound.

Feeling invisible, non-existent, so small,

Flowing like a speck of dust, drifting from view, unsure of it all,

Ego masks itself to allure you, a Pharaoh's palace to dwell,

Persuading you to serve the Pharaoh, a familiar captor's spell.

Break free from the grip of Egyptian gods, embrace the light,

Escape the clutches of the evil inclination, take flight.

Unshackle yourself from the chains of self-serving commandments,

Embrace the loving force of nature, find true liberation

And Understand that there is none else besides him, he is good and does good.

EMPTINESS

E mptiness engulfs you like the icy womb
Of a mother holding a lifeless child in her memory's tomb,

It hovers like a dark shroud, trapping you

In an invisible stranglehold of suffocating gloom.

Its chill pierces your bones, merging with your marrow,

Courses through veins like a shadowy blood cell,

Darkening your essence, bearing the message of nothingness.

Emptiness, an unwelcome lodger in your mind, now dwells.

It becomes an integral part of your very being,

And soon, it lays claim to your brainstem.

Loneliness, a ghostly whisperer, breathes chilling winds,

Claiming you for an eternity, your soul condemned.

Emptiness speaks a language only you can hear,

An understanding shared with your solitary self.

It Invades like an invisible force, creeping into your mind,

Spreading like hidden roots known to you alone, intertwined.

Emptiness knocks on your door like an uninvited guest,

When you're lonely and desperate for companionship.

With a hollow smile and open arms, it beckons you inside,

In that moment, life seems to escape you, a sinking ship forever.

Emptiness tears you from your true self,

Keeping you captive, estranged from familiar smiles.

Known joys, and the love that once defined you,

It clings like a parasite, feasting on misery and self-pity wiles,

Sucking you into the dust, preparing you for the cold grave,

Emptiness weaves a web of recurring thoughts,

Playing a deadly symphony, its eerie notes,

Vibrating through your spine in a vast, empty hall, suffocating as it haunts.

Emptiness drapes you in silence, a shroud of solitude,

Numbing your senses, rendering you invisible to the world.

You walk unnoticed, a ghost of your former self,

It disguises itself as a friendly companion, its allure unfurled.

Luring you toward the abyss of non-existence,

Emptiness, like a python, slowly suffocates your breath,

Strangling the life out of you, a gradual demise.

Revealing life's cunning and cruel other faces, leading to death.

It shadows you relentlessly, a constant reminder,

Of its existence and its power over your soul.

Confusion reigns as you traverse different dimensions,

Back and forth, lost within its relentless grip's toll.

Emptiness is an ocean swallowing you whole,

With waves that carry you high only to crash you down.

You watch life's stream flow by a tranquil river,

Yearning to chase it but numbed and detached, wearing a frown.

Tears flow silently, tracing pathways down your cheeks,

Awakening you as they saturate your shirt.

Acknowledging your sorrow for the first time,

You feel nothing, like a lifeless tree in a dark forest's despair,

Overgrown with poison ivy, abandoned, and forlorn,

The force of loneliness buries you beneath,

A mountain of anguish, rendering you insignificant,

But the ember of life still flickers within,

Fed by the damp leaves of loneliness, lacking warmth.

You must feed it differently, with dry kindlings of passion,

Twigs of joy, branches of cherished memories, and logs of life's worth.

Breathe in the breeze of acceptance; ignite the fire with the fuel of love,

In essence, to burn brightly once more.

Let it blaze; You are not dead; you are alive.

Crushed by life's cruelty but still here, life to explore.

Hear the fading music of life and rise.

A grain of sand, far from the beach tossed in the parking lot,

Free yourself from the torment, the chains Of destructive thoughts,

And the dark dungeon's grip.

Fight back and ask yourself, "How?"

Accept your life, converse with your pain, and don't let it slip.

Sip from the cup of coffee, and laugh at life's folly,

Make your own rules, and choose your own victories.

Once you've made peace with your pain,

Show it the door, for guests can not stay forever.

This is your house, your fire burning within,

And no one, not even loneliness, Can extinguish it again.

If loneliness knocks again someday,

Greet it with a cup of coffee and sit by the fire,

Chat like old friends, and then kindly escort it out.

It is your home, your fire, your life to live today,

And no one, nothing can dampen your spirit again.

2 O 2 2

IRAN

My beloved Iran, the beautiful mother of Persia, the queen of wisdom and grace,

Endured years of brutal barbarism, yet you never bowed to defeat's embrace.

You stood tall, guarding your land from Elbruz to Zagros, Koh-e Damavand to Dasht-e Kavir, and Dasht-e Lut to Bandar-e Abbas, protecting every inch of it.

You suffered rape, brutal beatings, and your cities were burned to the ground,

But you never bowed to the atrocities of barbarians throughout history.

My dear mother, Iran, each wrinkle on your face tells a story,

An impression of years of suppression and cruelty, your strength's allegory.

Let me feel your pain, so I may become one with it, understand your deep sorrow,

My strong mother, the lashes of tyranny over thousands of years, wounds to the marrow.

Your daughters groan, and their cries reach the gates of heaven, a river of grief they've borne,

The tombstones of children tremble with anger, piercing the hearts of humanity, wounds to the core.

The Karun River flows with the blood of your innocent children, its roars marking the path to freedom.

Unbind the braid of your white hair, let it shine like a diamond, a beacon, your emblem.

Every strand an unbreakable rope for your children to climb, fearlessly fight against the oppressive mullahs.

All your children need your strength to prevail, to fight for women, life, and freedom.

My Iran, my tolerant mother, patiently adapting, adjusting, knowing that the light will overcome the darkness one day,

Understand that all your children stand united, with one heart beating for your freedom.

Tears of blood well up at the corners of your eyes, my Iran, my dear mother,

The dark cloak of the mullahs has shadowed you for far too long,

But the bravery of your children blinds their wicked eyes,

The bodies of your children, women, and men, woven into the very fabric of your land.

The clouds are heavy with the impending storm of change,

The sky bursts, showering courage and sacrifice.

The rotting garments of the mullahs have darkened your land for 43 years,

How did you endure the unbearable stench of their existence?

The wicked took aim at your heart with sinful arrows,

But the unity of your children shielded you.

Your children melded into an unyielding fist to overthrow the savage mullahs.

Your freedom is within reach; the sacrifices of your children from every corner of your land will heal your deepest wounds.

My dearest mother, Iran, the diamond of Persia,the sun rising in the darkest monsoons.

Shine brightly with pride; Smile, for your children are united, their love for you unwavering,

We shall once again stand under the light of Ahura Mazda, our heritage and legacy savoring.

Honoring the legacy of Cyrus and the Charter of Human Rights, our shared goal.

AWE, LORD

Awe, Lord, each moment with you holds its own unique hue,

Each taste and each character is a reflects your divine view.

Every moment is a canvas of your exquisite art,

An Impression, a glimpse of your glory from the very start.

Awe, Lord, your fragrance lingers wherever I roam,

In each creation, your perfection finds a home.

Your love resides in every smile, each face,

Compassion dwells in every heart, in every loving embrace.

Awe, Lord, my love for you defies description's constraint,

Lost in a dimension where words find no paint.

A realm where shapes, sounds, and letters pale,

I stand in awe of your glory that keeps me on its trail.

In humility, I'm captivated by your majestic beauty,

Frozen in a timeless moment of divine duty.

Awe, Lord, when will I gaze upon your face?

In the darkness, I sit, devoid of fear's embrace.

Lost in a dimension with peace as my guide,

Navigating the wilderness of your love far and wide.

Crossing a bridge with no end in sight,

I journey on your path, Lifted by angels in the night.

I float, losing my sense of self's wrath,

I ascend through gates, inquiring for the secret word.

Only to find tears as the gatekeepers' message heard,

They open the gates, and I pass through, unbarred.

Light as a feather, a holy figure awaits me,

With love and affection, his face lights up, as it should be.

As if I've known him my whole life, a familiar being,

He beckons, saying "Come, my child, the journey was long".

His face illuminated as my senses prolonged,

Through the Garden of Eden, we venture along.

Moses, Gabriel, and angels soaring like a feather,

Violet dimensions with lions roaring together.

I pass through, invisible, without a sigh,

Arriving at a grand gate, my eyes behold, oh my!

A harp playing alone, King David's story told,

Angels soar above the garden's splendid unfold.

Yet, unwelcome, they say, I must turn away.

Exhaustion embraces my body, and the rain falls, leading the way.

I return to reality, both joyful and aloof,

Though I longed for the Kingdom of the Lord, the journey has been the truth.

I understand I still have work to afford.

Awe, Lord, tonight is a glorious nigh, your grace abounds,

Awe, Lord, a new day dawn, with your blessing, my heart resounds.

OH, MY LORD, MY KING

Oh, my Lord, my King,

To You, I extend my call, to You, my yearning heart is drawn,

For it is You, to whom I seek to cling, and whom I ever pursue.

Oh, my King, my Lord,

You are the one I require most, the absence of whom I fear,

For it is in You that my life finds purpose, and in You, I aspire to serve.

Oh, my Greatness, my Holiness,

I long to love You, to dedicate my entire existence to Your name,

And offer You each breath, to witness Your glorious being.

Oh, my Lord, my King,

I am but impoverished, a mere soul with nothing of my own,

Every gain I've known is a product of Your grace, my Lord.

All I possess is my existence, my heart, my soul; they are Yours to receive.

I am destitute, I am humble, but in loving You, I am rich.

As if the curtain has parted, I see clearly,

You are the guiding force of my existence and the entire universe.

My Lord, my King,

Am I deserving of Your love?

Am I worthy of being Your devoted servant?

Show me, teach me, guide me,

For without You, I am lost in a vast forest.

Call out to me, even if I am deaf,

For Your voice, I long to hear.

A SEARCH FOR MEANING

They speak of you as salvation and suffering,

The embodiment of light and darkness, perfection and imperfection,

Everything and nothing, silence and noise,

Joy and sorrow, vitality and duality.

You are the gentle cooing of a dove, the hum of the cricket,

The soft whisper of the wind, both healer and destroyer,

The tide that raises and pulls, a dance of stillness and motion,

The interplay of joy and disappointment, life and death.

Yet to me, you are the very breath of my life,

The guiding rope to my ascension, the comforting warmth I embrace,

The joy that permeates my soul, the truth I tirelessly seek,

A presence that dwells within all, and even within nothingness.

You stand as a constant, the essence of life itself,

If I were to peel existence layer by layer, you would remain.

In the petals of an orchid, I see your vibrant fibers,

Under the sun's benevolent rays, I feel your boundless compassion.

As I survey my surroundings, your presence envelops me,

Filling my heart and my very being to the brim.

The intensity of this connection stirs a desire to shout,

Tears of profound emotion cascade down my face.

Guide me in harnessing and channeling this sensation, solely to share,

Show me the path to offer it wholly unto you.

I feel unworthy of such an abundance of love, such a divine blessing,

Insignificant, like a mere speck of dust,

Yet, you love me. Despite my recurring sins, you grant forgiveness,

Clasping me close as though I were the most sacred of all.

You are my Lord, my life, my everything.

Words falter when I attempt to describe you,

For though you encompass the realm of good and bad,

I am enveloped solely by your unconditional love, your magnificence,

Your perfection, your beauty, your grace, your harmony, your balance,

Your truth, your honesty, and your boundless compassion.

TO MY MAGNIFICENT FRIENDS

You are the rope of my salvation,

The mirror of my perfection,

The reflection of darkness within light,

In you, I see my attributes, personalities, and characters,

The sparks of my shattered soul,

The dual piece, sharp, round, small, and large pieces.

You are the ladder to the Gmar Tikkun,

The temple of the Holy Shechina,

The Mikveh for my spiritual purification,

The field of bestowal,

The voice of holiness,

The impression of beauty,

The expression of love,

And the light within the darkness.

2020

DANCING WITH THE SHECHINA

Mother of all children, Queen of all domains,

I beheld a dancing flame, ablaze and bright,

Growing gracefully, in radiant refrains,

The blue light expanded, forming a bride of light.

She reached out, and I joined her with delight,

We danced skyward to celestial melodies' tunes,

As light as feathers, our spirits took flight,

To the East, West, South, North, under the moon.

We bowed and swayed like courtiers in a grand hall,

Our hands raised, held together, we spun, entwined,

Then, I released her hand, saw the Shechina's call,

A radiant bride, in white, in light, she climbed.

No substance to ground her, she danced with grace,

Higher she twirled until she despaired,

My heart rejoiced for she'd found her place,

With her beloved, divine love finally declared.

EMBRACE OF DARKNESS

I behold the shroud of darkness encasing me,

Concealing my very essence, an obsidian embrace.

I willingly descend into its depths,

Let it chase, possess me, draw me into its core, I see.

Darkness, an extension of my soul, I now perceive,

No longer do I fear its murky domain.

In its imperfection, I find my reprieve,

The beauty within, a revelation, my gain.

Silence ushers in peace, tranquil, and complete,

Beside You, all else fades into the night.

Embracing lack and void, a familiar feat,

I see the beauty in the absence of light.

I am nothingness, Identity nullified,

Enshrouded in Your glory, deep within the dark.

Relief in the void, one authority,

Goodness prevails as I embark on this sacred journey.

Life and purpose within the night, I discern,

A hidden wisdom concealed within the abyss.

Oneness in the evening where the light does yearn,

Playing a divine game of hide-and-seek pure bliss.

Revelation of your perfection, joy unfurls.

Your love envelopes the darkness, complete.

In your authority, merciful revealed,

No fear remains when you goodness I greet.

IN SEARCH OF HOME

Master of Universe, you beheld your people's doom, untenable,

Our faces were painted with the despair of impending ruin,

You felt our hearts smashed and bleeding,

Heard our cries of anguish in the dark, our hearts consumed.

You touched our pain, excruciating and dire,

Felt the torment of Egyptian lashes, bloodied and scarred .

Our prayers, broken, you heard, Our spirits on fire,

With mercy, you saved us, leading us from that wretched life.

Now, in the desert, a brutal journey unfolds,

Morning breezes pound us with grains of sand, like shattered glass.

The day's heat confounds, in confusion, we hold,

And the cold night's fear grips us as we release of your grasp.

The desert's bitterness tempts a return, a regressive trace,

Whispering winds convey truths we can't quite hear.

Hot sands evoke memories of that brutal slavery's embrace,

Storms pull us into chaos, a vortex of doubt, a place of fear.

Why do we feel wounded, defeated, and alone?

Numb in our weary garments, swinging like a pendulum wild,

Dejected, distant from our beloved, our own,

Insignificant in this desert, why this homesick yearning?

AWAKENING

Awakening from a deep slumber's embrace,

Emerging from the depths of a rotten swamp's trace,

Freed from cage-like thoughts' confines,

I transform into a lover butterfly seeking the light that shines.

Like an orphan child, I find my long-lost kin,

Reunited with my parents, love's sweet embrace, a welcome win.

A wondrous seeker, at home, I begin,

A wild flame in the darkness, I dance with grace,

I sense belonging to a greater cause, a purpose.

Connected to the root of trees, the moon's gentle lights, the sun's surface,

Joined in the galaxy, part of the cosmic circus,

Intoxicated by the Creator's love, I take flight.

I shed my mortal shell, my identity's heavy weight,

Abandoning the confines of my ethnicity, it's never too late,

In awe of the magnificent Creator, I contemplate.

A soul reborn in boundless serenity, a journey so great.

59

THE DANCE OF CONNECTION

In our rendezvous, dear friends, let us transcend

Divorce our identities, shed self-importance's weight

Break the chains of self-love; let it not contend

Lock emotional baggage away in the closet, isolate.

Leave behind fancy garments and dirty glasses

Pull aside the mirage's curtain, broaden our view

Open our hearts, dispense with painted faces

Permit the dirt to present itself, revealed and true.

See only the spark of the Creator's light

Find greatness in our friends, selfless and free

Embrace humility and non-judgment in our sight

Unite with love and compassion, a boundless sea.

Be venerable and transparent as we aspire

Towards the center of connection, as one, we stand,

May the Creator's light, a refining fire

Pierce desires, probe deficiencies, and expand hearts.

Let the reforming light dance and joyfully touch

Our souls awaken us to a sacred brotherhood, sisterhood

Remember, there is none else besides him; he is good, and does good, in His truth, we've understood.

THE WHISPER OF THE SHECHINA

A voice whispered in my ear during the Shabbat candle's glow,
"You have forgotten me, abandoned me," it said, low.

Deep in my heart, I sensed the Shechina's presence,

Frozen, gazing into the distance, a soul in penitence.

I beheld a dark, stony castle in the misty shroud,

My queen, Shechina, on her throne, regal and proud.

Her kingdom, a realm beneath a greedy, dark cloud,

In command but defeated by a beast, grief unbowed.

Her face, hair, and body were covered in the dust of human sin,

Ensnared in a giant spider's web, awaiting a bitter end.

Eyes fixed on the distant horizon, a solemn grin,

Expressing the betrayal of her children, a loss to comprehend.

I felt her pain, the agony of losing to the Sitra Achra's might,

A ray of light danced, transforming her into a forgotten mother's plight.

Sorrow for separation, her children's choice in flight,

Abandoned, forgotten, left in the depths of night.

Shame washed over me as I realized my part,

Among the children who'd forsaken, an aching heart.

Tears rolled, frozen in time, worlds apart,

A heavy heart, as if, for the first time, I knew my true art.

My spirit transcended as if my essence she'd condemned,

Yet, in that moment, I grasped the depths of my true name.

Note: Sitra Achra=The side of impurity

IN SEARCH OF THE DIVINE

Lord, your name echoes as tears fall upon my pillow,

Reciting Shema Israel, I feel the vibration of your love throughout my being.

My love for you never wanes, but only strengthens.

The memory of our union is the most precious gem I possess.

In the cold dungeon of reality,

I yearn for your love with desperation.

I know nothing beyond loving you,

Wandering, knocking on doors as an orphan seeking you,

Passing by countless faceless and nameless souls,

Greeting them with a smile, yet knowing I do not belong there.

I am a sinner, but you still shower me with love, I feel it in my bones.

I am fearful, for I am everything but nothing like you.

Shame engulfs me for neglecting your path and straying from your holiness,

Yet, even in darkness, I feel your presence near.

Loving you courses through my veins, circulating joyfully.

It is etched into my very existence, every fiber of my being.

I know nothing else but to love you,

Since the moment my soul shattered into pieces, I yearned for you.

In the wilderness, I cried for our union,

I yelled your name repeatedly in my head.

I searched tirelessly, turning over every stone,

Passing by faceless and nameless people, feeling disconnected from life.

Your compassion shielded me from life's cruelty,

I thank you with every breath I take.

My longing for you, my beloved Master, knows no bounds.

Your love is the only reality that exists.

My heart beats to the melody of your name,

There is no one and nothing but you.

I am nothing, no one without you;

I am nonexistent without you.

My Lord, reveal your face; reveal your face,

I know you are with me in every blink of an eye, in every breath of my life.

Loving you is life itself, a journey I must complete.

Show me how to serve you, be your lover and partner,

For life without you is but a form of death.

Note: Shema Israel = A Jewish prayer

CHRYSALIS REALMS

We're drawn into our private worlds, like caterpillars

Encased within a chrysalis of our own minds, with no escape.

Each one has cultivated its own chrysalis,

With distinct hues and qualities that define its shape.

Within each chrysalis, humanity's world unfurls,

Operating separately, each precisely as designed.

Each of us narrates a unique story as a writer or storyteller,

Portraying different roles as actors, actresses, directors, or playwrights.

Each of us composes diverse melodies as a musicians or composers,

Dancing to the rhythms that flow as a choreographer and dancers.

Our artistic brush strokes paint varied pictures,

With colors, textures, and expressions enhancing our answer.

In the vast human world, countless chrysalises reside,

Some transparent, some rigid, others coarse or dark, as they exist.

This is what we comprehend, the illusion of humankind,

Disconnected from its source, from the divine, from the ultimate.

In this illusion, one may assume they are a deity,

The creator of their own world, separate and unique.

We excel at shaping separate realms apart from one another,

Disengaged from the universal masculine and feminine, a cosmic mystique.

2 0 1 7

ENLIGHTENMENT

Amidst years of pain and sorrow, life couldn't crush my vibrant spirit.

I believed that through suffering, salvation would be found.

I embraced each pain, without complaint,

Endured it with a sense of superiority,

Trapped for so long under the spell of ego, I had forgotten my true essence.

Once the facade of my ego shattered into pieces,

I gazed into my eyes and recognized my true self.

Life's energy smiled back at me, tender and compassionate,

Tears flowed like a joyous stream on my face.

With closed eyes, I grasped that suffering and salvation were illusions,

Only pure existence, pure perfection in the universe, remained.

I'd always looked outward in search of answers,

Desiring to feel the truth of my existence.

I knew the life I lived was not mine, not real,

There was more to this existence than my sinful role.

I disconnected from the life energy within me,

Hoping to one day achieve true salvation, to fly free like a butterfly.

How mistaken I was!

I failed to see my ego's dominion over my world.

I passed through life as a faceless wanderer,

An orphan child, a lost soul without direction,

An aimless traveler with no destination,

An intoxicated seeker without bounds.

I couldn't see the truth, feel my essence,

How could I, a faceless woman lost in a mysterious world?

Staring at the mirror, I saw only the reflection of my ego,

My spirit cried out, and my soul was in torment,

My heart whispered I was in divine presence,

Grace within me shielding me from evil's horror.

My spirit urged me to wake from these lies and seek the truth.

It nodded gently, pulled me within, and embraced me with love.

The voice of my spirit, the force that looked inward, hypnotized me,

All I saw was the mask of my ego hovering over my existence,

Mesmerized, the ego proclaimed, "I am GOD."

I was hijacked by ego, disconnected from truth,

Now I know with all my heart, THE UNIVERSE IS IN ME,

I understand, GOD IS ME.

How could I have been ignorant of my existence for so long?

Disconnected from my inner self, devoid of compassion,

Living in an illusion, believing I was GOD.

All I can do now is repent, "PLEASE TRUTH, ELIMINATE THE FALSE."

Layers of ego's lies entrapped me,

Life exposed me to the cruel world of humankind,

I endured immense pain, and finally, I died.

Who am I, the one who endured so much agony?

The answer is my ego, my distorted perception.

I woke from a deep slumber, Now, I feel the ocean breeze,

God's caress on my face, My heart overflows with love and compassion.

I believe in the divine existence in every breath I take,

In the warmth of the sun's embrace, In the beauty of each face, fortunate or not.

I am liberated from the cage of the material world,

Reborn, connected to the divine light, grounded yet floating in every direction.

I am reborn, again.

ECHOES OF THE MIND

Memories hang like portraits on the walls of your mind,

Now and then, you cast your gaze upon them.

You pause; emotions surge through your heart,

Beating rapidly, known and unknown feelings wash over you,

As if you're reliving those moments once again,

Or perhaps you sense nothing, as if they are lifeless images.

You journey through the archives of an emotionless life,

Memories: a bittersweet taste of existence.

Here and there, you steal glances at them,

Suddenly, familiar and unfamiliar flavors burst into your tongue,

Or is it tasteless, as if all your taste buds have all but vanished,

As though you've lost the capacity to savor life.

Attachments drape your fragile heart with weight,

Any moment, they can shatter it and bring sorrow.

Possession is akin to a chain, constraining your free will and true purpose.

You may believe that without it, you are adrift, rootless and disconnected,

Or you might feel liberated, as if you're as free as the air, unbound by earthly constraints.

Attachment resembles an unhealthy relationship craving attention,

Hijacking your true self and identity.

Feelings express your destructive thoughts, repressed desires,

Unwanted nightmares, unfulfilled dreams, and broken hearts.

Feelings are the breath that infuses life into your character,

Connecting with your divine soul, touching the truth within.

Feel the divine energy coursing through you,

The true force of life, an unseen light like never before,

Or deny its existence and continue in a world of nightmares.

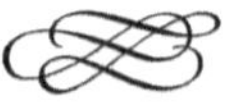

A SOUL'S PLEA

Is it you who enters my dreams,

Whispers my name with yearning, and dances alongside me?

Is it you I've loved so profoundly in my heart?

Have you belonged to me since the inception of my existence?

Is it you who awakens my soul, living in my thoughts and breathing through me from the very start?

Is it truly you, the one I've ceaselessly sought?

Help me, for my soul yearns to escape my earthly vessel and unite with you.

Guide me in finding my path, lost and without direction.

Restore my courage to embrace life once more.

Assist me, for my soul longs to soar again,

To live with love, to love you till the end of time.

Aid me in recovering the joy that has been my essence since birth.

Help me rediscover my true self, lost in the unknown realm.

Heal me and allow me to dance with my beloved before the flame of passion expires.

Guide me to witness you, for my life force wanes before my very eyes.

Breathe life into my nostrils, revive me, for I am departing this world without you, and that is a great sorrow.

LONGING AND NOSTALGIA

All my dreams, my hopes, and regrets entwined,

In what words, with what message, and voice defined,

To call for you, yearn, and touch your heart's grace,

Seek your eyes, embrace your warmth, find my place.

With love, I worship, with regrets, I remember,

I wait for your return, for one more day to tender,

Aching for your presence, your moments to borrow,

In this longing and nostalgia, I find solace, not sorrow.

2014

INTOXICATED BY YOUR PRESENCE

I'm intoxicated by your presence, your kiss, your touch,

My heart syncs with the rhythm of your breathing.

My blood rushes to my once-broken heart, healing its pieces.

When you gaze into my eyes, I see a familiar face from ages past,

And I feel the warmth of your tender love in your stare.

In your eyes, I get lost in time and presence in a single moment.

You hold me in your arms, and we become one,

Your touch upon my face feels like a soft breeze from heaven,

As we dance together in the sweet liberation of our souls.

OBSERVER OF LIVES

I 've stood beside you, watching your life unfold before my eyes.

I've witnessed your struggles, fears, and your broken heart's cries,

I've seen your dreams, desires, and moments of joy, and despair,

The times you felt you both belonged and didn't, I'm aware.

I observed your shattered dreams, your heart's silent bleed,

Your moments of confusion, like secrets you'd never heed.

Your life played out like a movie before my eyes,

Unaware that you played in every scene, where your true self lies.

I smiled as your spirit danced, carefree, unconfined,

In and out of the movie, like there's no concept or defined line.

No sense of belonging, no awareness of time and space,

I watched your hand cover your face, heard your sobs embrace.

Tears flowed like a river down your cheeks, like a gentle stream,

Your soul yearning for the truth, for understanding, like a distant dream.

I witnessed your growth, your failures, your triumphs, and your journey's grace,

As life's story unfolded, a unique and beautiful embrace.

DIVINE AWAKENING

I know the Lord's unconditional love breathed life into me when I was fading.

It was the Lord's hand that touched my soul, setting it free.

His compassion lifted my spirit from the brink of destruction,

The whisper of His grace elevated me from the darkest pit.

I know it was the touch of the Lord that stirred me awake.

With His strength and courage, I faced the darkness head-on,

I buried the past, looked forward, and knew the Lord had always been by my side.

2014

IN THE ABYSS OF LOSS

My heart bleeds as you drift away from me,

Tears flow like a river, only heaven weeping in sympathy.

My aura shatters, and life departs with you,

Darkness, emptiness, and cold creep into my soul,

A frozen spirit lost in time and space.

Thoughts race toward the unknown and nothingness.

My journey flows like a lifeless river, I watch it emotionlessly.

I see sunlight, yet I feel cold and smell darkness,

Days appear gloomy, as if life shares my sorrow.

Flowers bloom everywhere, but I only see death,

My soul seems pierced on a crucifix, numb and breathless.

My spirit flakes away in the encroaching darkness,

While the light within me dims and fades.

I drown deeper in this dark, cold pit,

My hand reaches desperately, my spirit calls for help,

81

But only darkness and emptiness respond from below.

Time bears me forward, life burying me with cold dirt,

I sob silently to the heavens, pleading for release.

My gaze is fixed on the distant, misty road,

My spirit stares, unblinking as if witnessing the end of my pitiful existence.

You drift away from me in this life.

I cry out your name with all my might, but only silence echoes back.

My sorrow rushes to embrace my bleeding heart,

My shadow shatters and washes away in the rain.

Pain squeezes my being as my life chases after you.

Colors fade, and life is painted with a glassy tint of gray.

Emptiness worms its way into my heart, draining love and joy.

Music stops, and silence orchestrates the void.

People remain strangers with faceless forms running aimlessly,

Friends and family's voices mute, their words lost in the wind.

The rainbow shatters into pieces, showering my vision with gray inks.

Flowers wither as a cursed shadow passes by.

I'm lost, without you, I am nothing.

Come back to me, for I yearn for you desperately.

It's been too long, and I no longer recognize myself,

I feel like a forgotten ghost, a mere specter of who I once was.

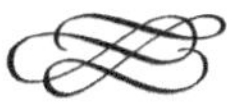

EMBRACING LIFE

I won't allow sorrow, guilt, and fear to crucify my soul,

Negativity won't drain the life from within me,

Sadness won't quench the spark of life in my heart,

Pain won't find a refuge within my heart.

I won't surrender to nothingness nor to emptiness within my soul,

Sorrow won't sever me from my true essence,

Time and space won't halt my journey; life must persist.

The era of weeping has ended, and I now wear a smile,

The days of sorrow are behind me, replaced by pure delight,

Mourning has surrendered to rebirth,

The dark cloud has dissipated from my mind and aura,

As the sun shines down on me, I rejoice in the celebration of life.

AWAKENING TO LOVE

I'm in the process of healing in the present, unaware of my own existence,

Intoxicated with ego, your love mends my soul's persistence.

I'm ailing from a potion of deception, your kisses break the spell,

Contaminated by revenge, you embrace my heart with forgiveness so well.

Blinded by hatred, you bless me with compassion's grace,

Burning like a candle in the dark, your light brightens my life's embrace.

I'm in despair, haunted by loneliness, your love unites my heart as one,

Rejecting my innocence, you project your holiness; healing has begun.

Still, I fight and search in denial for your love, unaware it's everywhere I go,

Everywhere I turn, your presence in my heart does gently glow.

LONGING FOR REVELATION

I'm entranced by your tranquil peace,
Your love engulfs me in a sweet release.
I bask in the comfort your presence does bring,
Fearless in the embrace of your truth's powerful wing.
In love with your compassion's endless grace,
Tears of joy flow when I glimpse your face.
Your sound brings tranquility to my soul,
And your beauty leaves me in awe, feeling whole.
I'm liberated in the glow of your glory's light,
Your existence knows me, makes everything right.
I'm cheerful, uplifted by your melodious song,
A child in your nurturing, where I truly belong.
But why, I wonder, are you hiding from me,
When I ache for your presence and long to be free?

YEARNING FOR DIVINE CONNECTION

My Lord, release me from my delusions, my dark perceptions,

Lift me from the mire of doubt's disorienting directions.

Set me adrift in the boundless ocean of your love's embrace,

As I see your beauty in every flower, in every space.

I sense your presence in each breath I gently inhale,

In the warmth of the sun's benevolent, golden trail.

Your compassion radiates in the gentle moonlight's stare,

I am immersed in your peace, in tranquil, silent prayer.

When you revealed the mirror, my existence's truth shone through,

Enlightened by you, restless thoughts I now subdue.

I bear your attributes, love's flame within me does grow,

Your presence consumes me, your love does enthrall.

Grant me the chance to build a temple for worship's consecration,

To serve as your devoted servant in endless dedication.

Permit me to be a lover, celebrating your divine grace,

To light a candle, illuminating your sacred space.

My Lord, every time my heart calls your sacred name,

You are there, an eternal, unwavering flame.

My tears cascade down, in joy, love's sweet embrace,

As your affection envelops me, in your eternal grace.

SEARCH FOR YOUR PRESENCE

Where have you been, my Lord, all these years and times?

Reveal yourself to me; I'm losing my sight in these climbs.

Take my spirit; I'm withering in fear's embrace,

Find me, for I'm lost in the labyrinth of doubt's maze.

Lift me to the Garden of Eden's serenity,

Free me from these relentless, recurring thoughts, unendingly.

2010

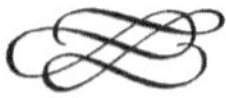

IN UNITY WITH THE DIVINE

When I detach from life's worldly strife,

I discover life itself, anew and rife.

In life's embrace, I find my very core,

And in that journey, I find you, my Lord.

I am love, and I am beloved, intertwined,

In unity, you and I, the divine combined.

2010

THE ALCHEMY OF LOVE

Let love flourish within, the ego shall fade,

A key to your heart's cage, love's serenade.

Embrace its gentle touch, let its attributes flow,

Love's silent dialogue, peace it shall bestow.

A smile from love, igniting compassion's fire,

A kiss on your forehead, your soul to inspire.

THE HEALING OF LOVE'S PRESENCE

With your presence in my heart, disease is set to cease,

Leaving only the fragrance of love in its release.

No more darkness, only sunshine's radiant ray,

No more hatred, just forgiveness to hold sway.

With your presence in my heart, despair finds no place,

Leaving only compassion, a guiding grace.

2010

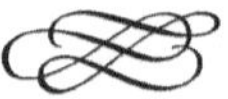

IN THE SHATTERED MIRROR'S GAZE

I found you within a shattered mirror, marred by my own vice,
In the broken fragments, sharp and rough, I paid the price.
I embraced the lost faith of countless nights and endless days,
Entwined with the tempting chill, I danced in grace's embrace.

2010

WHISPERS OF THE HEART

My heart aches for you, as you free me from agony's chain,

Yelling in silence, in your peace, I find my gain.

Begging for your return, though you never did depart,

My heart bleeds for you, healing my wounded heart.

THE ETERNAL PRESENCE

You are my shadow, though your benign light,

Defies the transient nature of shadows in sight.

My shadow may fade, but you shall remain,

You are my soul, my love, my life's endless reign.

Yet life itself can't encompass your existence's domain,

My life may cease, but you still unshakably remain.

You are my silent voice, my peace, and my breath,

Even my breath can't unveil your essence beneath.

Though my breath may wane, you'll forever sustain,

You are my beloved, my heartbeat, all I possess, in your reign.

But my heartbeat falls short to fathom your true name,

My heart may still, yet you persist, the same.

You are my love, my past, present, and future's mission,

Even my vision can't grasp your ultimate definition.

Though my vision may fade, you'll continue to reign,

In your eternal presence, I shall forever remain.

PASSING STRANGER

A stranger, bearing a lantern, traversed the frigid winter alley of my life.

Our eyes met, our lips intertwined,

And suddenly, he became the unfamiliar face of my dreams.

The alley twisted, and I felt transformed.

The sun emerged, casting a hopeful light on tomorrow.

In my dark haven, we converged, molded in love,

But abruptly, I awoke from the sweetest dream.

Time halted, the sunset, and dark clouds veiled the sky.

His countenance dissolved as night surrendered,

Sadly, he was but a fleeting passerby, a stranger in passing.

Between us is an expanse, a chasm of space.

In the realm of love, I would have worshiped you entirely.

I could have cherished every passing moment of my life,

Believed in you, even in the realm of the unrealistic

In love, I'd have adored you without question,

Believed you, despite the incredulity of my beliefs,

Summarized my life within your presence.

At times and places, I'd have instantly merged with you,

Shared your sorrows, be your confidant for the morrow

But alas, I bore witness to the sunset of your life today,

Regrettably, you aged, you withered.

In the privacy of my own eyes, I perceived the confusion of detachment.

Miles apart, I saw you slice off from my soul,

I closed my eyes, tears flowing like a river,

My soul withered, my heart lamenting in desolation.

In my dreams, I kissed you, your lips framed upon the wall of my heart.

The frame shattered, and my heart wept once more.

In my dreams, I kissed you, bidding farewell with memories.

I trembled, eyes wide open,

Yearning to revisit our memories in the darkness and solitude of my dreams.

But alas, I witnessed the sunset of your life today.

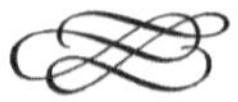

FROZEN MOMENTS

I walked through the icy, cold alley of time,

As winter's grip was fading away.

The snow turned dark and gray,

Faceless snowmen deep in slumber.

The air was heavy with cold,

I merely passed through the alley, dark and frigid.

Familiar faces with vacant stares.

Then, a stranger with a lantern approached,

And in his gaze, everything changed.

The sun burst forth, the snow melted,

Waters flowed, and streams converged.

Flowers bloomed, nightingales sang a familiar tune,

The alley transformed with unimaginable delight,

He held my hands and kissed my lips,

A warmth surged within,

I resurrected and blossomed anew,

Blood rushed through my veins,

My heart raced, and my eyes saw life's beauty.

I stood, stunned, fixated,

My gaze locked in his dreamy eyes,

He transported me to another realm

As if in a dream, everything reshaped.

At that moment, I felt love, love reborn, and long-forgotten emotions resurfaced.

I recalled buried love, its scent, its taste, its essence,

All dissipated by time, leaving no trace behind.

Yet now, I know the feeling,

But fear has taken hold of my being.

Afraid of falling in love once more,

Consumed by the fiery flames of passion,

I'm terrified to surrender my heart and soul,

Worried he might leave at love's zenith,

Fearing the unpredictable power of love,

Anxious, he might be a fleeting passerby.

1994

ETERNAL FLAMES OF LOVE

I remembered you in shades of blue, azure, purple,

Yellow, red, and the fiery orange glaze.

I endured the burning heat of that fiery fire.

I noticed how you vanished like scorching flames in the darkness of the passing moment.

I heard you, a desperate shout from the dark ashes,

Yearning to catch the flame and rejoin the fire.

I set you ablaze, and you ignited, rising high,

Crying out to the heavens above.

And so, I remained beneath the ashes,

Allowing you to burn brightly for eternity,

All for the sake of love.

1992

RESCUED BY THE DIVINE LIGHT

I sat in a dark, damp corner,

Tears welled up in my eyes,

Shock rendering my body cold and numb.

I felt the moisture in the air seeping in deeply,

With tear-filled eyes, I raised my hands to the heavens.

Trembling, I cried out, "Lord, find me in this solitude."

Light illuminated the sky, and it thundered,

I heard a voice reverberating through the air, saying, "I have heard you.

I will guide you home; I will free you from this cruel world.

1991

FAREWELL TO THE FUTURE

I rest upon the lifeless bench of existence,

  Autumn's image of death hangs within my heart's hall.

I sense my fading as quivering leaves descend,

The cruel chill bites at my fragile form.

With feeble hands, I shield my face

To spare it from life's lashes' cruel sting,

Yet, death's mournful howls fill the air,

My trembling hands pressed close to my ears in vain defense.

No one beckons me, no one perceives me here

On this soulless bench of existence,

No one arrives with a guiding lantern,

No one believes in the unthinkable demise of my life.

I gaze into the distant corner with a mix of longing and despair,

Hoping perhaps to see him once more,

Yet, he will not come, he shall not return,

Leaving me to confront the relentless march of time alone.

The biting cold stings my eyes, closing them in surrender,

Yet, I dare not slumber, for fear of seeing him there.

In this forsaken corner of life's unforgiving realm,

I must bid farewell to the future, for he shall not come,

Leaving me to endure these painful moments in solitude.

1991

SILENT DESPERATION

I yearn to shout with all my might, to let the pain within my heart take flight,

Yet, I am bound, burdened by life's autumn's untimely start, my cries suppressed, out of sight.

As the final leaf of hope gently falls, I too shall fade from view,

Unnoticed by those who roam, unaware of my inner blue.

But I love you with my heart's entirety, my soul, my essence so divine,

Never have I been so ensnared by love's potent line.

Rescue me, my savior, or release me from this love's firm hold,

I'm weary of this strife, it's time for my freedom, or so I've been told.

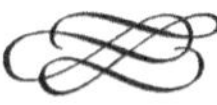

DESPAIR IN THE SILENCE OF LIFE

I found myself drowning in life's brutal silence,

As I stared at the putrid swamp of betrayal's defiance.

Then, your shadow drew near, and I sensed your presence,

My gaze was hurried, unable to focus, in my own defense.

You began speaking of tomorrows and hope so bright,

Yet your words seemed hollow in the dim of my mind's night.

You reached for me, your hands framed my face, seeking a kiss,

But your touch, like sharp claws, brought an unwelcome abyss.

I yearned to scream, to cry, to break free from your grasp,

Wishing for a single red rose on my final path.

That your name never etched my destiny's book,

That your love had never found my heart's hidden nook.

I wished I'd never heard your enchanting voice in the lonely night's embrace,

Or laid eyes upon you in that haunting, misty space.

Perhaps then, despair wouldn't hold me tight,

And I'd escape the clutches of this endless night.

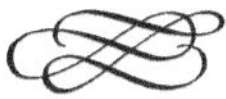

CITY OF MOURNING

A city of mourning, where life's death is deeply felt,
A place of emptiness, where love's absence is heart-wrenching.

Silent streets reverberate with the void of existence,

The cry of death, a haunting scream in the air.

Nights filled with the anxiety of waiting,

Endless and excruciating, the relentless passage of time.

Faces bear expressions of shock and overwhelm,

Hearts shattered in this dark, desolate existence.

Here, the last breaths are drawn,

Words laden with hatred and despair,

Endless roads leading to nowhere in this desolation.

Everything draped in mourning for the loss of life.

Silence lingers, the void of living,

The solitary dance of a clock's lone hand,

Droplets fall like echoes in this abyss of stillness.

In the silence, the void witnesses non-existence.

All mourn, all voice their grievances,

Their sorrows speak of pain, separation from their true selves,

Despair reigns as they long for a home free from sorrow's grip.

Blasphemous words are spoken, a disconnect from the divine,

In this corner of the world, the Lord is no longer invoked,

The creator is forgotten in this collective mourning,

No hands rise to the sky in prayer or repentance.

Life has transformed into something unrecognizable,

No longer the life of humankind,

It's a day of distance, where the gap between us seems insurmountable.

Our souls ache for connection, unity, a shared consciousness.

My life today, your life today, all feel so far away,

The distance is not just between points or lines,

But between two souls, two hearts, two human beings,

Life has become an alien concept, distant from humanity.

WHISPERS OF LIFE

Listen to the raindrops' gentle patter,

They murmur tales of nights filled with waiting's bitter chatter.

Observe the autumn leaves as they gently fall,

Their descent reminds us life is a journey, change embraces all.

Watch the sun dip by a tranquil shore, I

t whispers of fleeting moments, forever to be no more.

Witness the dawn on a misty morn,

A new beginning, with each sunrise reborn.

Gaze at the candle's flickering flame,

It speaks of love's mad fire, burning all the same.

Dwell in the voice of silence profound,

It murmurs of stillness, where nothing's found.

See a woman's face, barefoot in the rain's sweet kiss,

A story of breaking boundaries, of finding boundless bliss.

And now, lend an ear to me,

As I unravel the enigmatic, the unknown, you'll see,

Discussing life's riddles, being a riddle, a mystery,

In a world that often feels like a grand history.

1991

STRANGER IN THE NIGHT

You embarked on a journey, and I, in painful anticipation, waited,

Time drags along as if the clock's hands slumber, oblivious to me.

Set adrift on a voyage, I'm haunted by the torment of your absence,

Lonely nights find me lost in the darkness, awaiting your return.

Time crushes me cruelly, as if the rusted chariot of fate moves relentlessly,

Others dance their intricate lives, unaware of the void you've left behind.

Yet, your name repeats in my moments of longing,

Yearning for your presence, your embrace, your soothing voice.

In these moments, your beautiful image weaves my wounded soul,

Bringing tears to my parched lips, I waited for you, painfully waiting.

When you departed, the city's cherry blossoms burst into bloom,

A strange spectacle of joy and celebration, a world I couldn't join.

The blossoms withered and died with our parting,

And when I returned, the city exuded the scent of death.

Sorrow and despair cast a shadow over the streets,

The suffocating darkness echoed with howling winds.

With a voice quivering with agony, I cried out,

"I'll be back next year to see you with the one who journeyed away."

The nightingales sang of spring, invoking your name and mine,

In the verses of lovers, but I had no response, my tongue tied.

I watched them in mourning, their melodies fading into the distance,

Beseeching them not to leave me alone, yearning for their return.

They left me in silence, departing like fleeting shadows,

In this silence, I grasped the truth of life's ebb and flow,

The belief in existence is not the same as being.

The wait has ended; an unknown traveler, in the form of my beloved, has returned,

Delivering me the gift of shattered hope, the fractured visage of happiness.

He brought me autumn as a parting gift, whispering the language of love's eventual end.

Not the traveler I knew, not my weary lover; just a stranger in the night.

1991

MY WILL

I yearn to ascend, to reach the pinnacle's height,

Not just traverse the Earth's surface, chained to their spite.

My wings crumble beneath their weighty boots,

For they may aim arrows of hatred, shooting to pollute.

Even if I soar high above, they may still try,

Forever breaking my wings, in their hatred's fiery cry.

But I can't remain, watching time stagnate,

I must take flight, embrace a new fate.

No, I won't be consumed by their archaic ways,

Not perpetuate backwardness and prejudice as life's phase.

I won't linger here, returning to days of slavery and spite,

I am a free river, meant to flow, even in the darkest night.

I'll surge forward, quench the arid land's thirst,

Revive withered roots, nurture blooms that have been cursed.

I am the liberated voice, refusing fanaticism's call,

A beacon of hope, slicing through darkness to freedom's thrall.

Yes, I am a free woman,

Breaking chains of intolerance to embrace liberty's beacon.

I have the right to soar, though they fixate on me with disdain,

For their scrutiny is like loathsome mice, and I am not the same.

Their ways are not mine, we're strangers through and through,

I refuse their legacy, for what's graceful to them is disgraceful to my view.

I'm not one of them in heart, spirit, thoughts, or deeds,

Won't perpetuate their decaying legacy for future seeds.

I won't blindly follow ancestors' decrees,

I must fly high, to escape their painful freeze,

Their obscured thoughts, oppressive deeds, the unjust truth they please.

I believe in myself, I believe in my cause,

I'm a free woman, breaking free from their unjust laws.

My birthright is freedom, I won't live in submission,

Won't tolerate injustice, it's not in my vision.

I will not let them crush my spirit with their iron boots,

My birthright is to live freely as a woman, that's the truth.

I won't endure their injustice, no, I won't bow,

I must fly without fear, from a single dot I'll draw.

O, my beloved pen, O, my faithful paper,

Witness to my memories, expressions, I won't taper.

I embark on this journey, starting from this humble place,

Hoping to find lines of progress, freedom, love's grace.

If my voice falters before the start, let it be known,

Another woman like me will continue, seeds sown.

Tell the world, "This is a woman who writes,

Fosters a culture of progress, shaping new, brilliant lights."

I'll soar to the highest peaks, awakening conscience and love,

Unity, liberation, and the peace we dream of.

PREGNANT WITH LOVE

I carried your love within me from the moment you said goodbye,

As you vanished into the shroud of night, my heart let out a sigh.

You departed, but in my moments, I sought you near,

I glimpsed you in the wind's wings and followed without fear.

I called your name, singing it in my memory's song,

Yet my trembling voice faded as a hungry wolf howled strong.

You didn't hear me as I pursued you, swift and light,

Till I found you on the turbulent ocean's tide.

I shouted your name, beseeching you from the waves so wide,

But fate's cruel hand had left your ears denied.

Seabirds filled the void with their clamorous cry,

I cried your name, sinking in the waves, oh my, oh my.

Relentlessly, I pursued until a mermaid I did meet,

I whispered the tale of love's conception, oh so sweet.

She cleaved the heart of the sea, my guide and confidant,

But alas, it was too late, my dear, my love, my want.

I found you resting in the unfeeling, stony embrace of the grave,

I implored with mournful wails, my heart's cry, so brave.

I called to the grave, "Open your heart or set him free,

Take me with you, release him, or share him with me."

No answer, so I dug my fingers deep into the earth's hold,

Toiled upon her callous heart, with love untold.

She laughed, a hearty laugh, and looked me in the eye,

"You're a fool, unaware of love's carousel ride."

"He left you ensnared in sin, love's fleeting game,

Elevated you to passion's peak, then snuffed love's flame.

Made you but a dalliance, left you far behind,

Now you ask me to set him free, unbind."

I cried, "Have mercy, for I'm pregnant with his love's art,

Either leave him to me or take me in his stead from the start."

Then a loathsome worm emerged, declaring him no more,

His spirit had flown, his body now in my heart's core.

To say farewell, you must kiss me, my plea so deep,

I poured dirt on my head and face, my sorrow to keep.

A gust of wind shook me, sardonic look on her face,

She sat by my side, grip on my hand, in disgrace.

She said, "Why did you bury yourself like this, my dear?

Now, you're gone too," with a voice so clear.

It was then I cried out, "O cruel grave, so stern,

You said I was unaware of love's carousel's turn."

"Is this love's zenith where he left me alone?

Did you take him away when love finally shone?

The fire of longing consumed him, hope did burn,

Is this love's carousel's turn? No, it's tyranny, I discern.

WITH YOU

Transforming night into morning, hand in hand we go,

Our paths converge, ascending together in a gentle flow.

Yearning for love's sweet embrace, hearts aglow,

From the horizon, we recall sunsets of long ago.

We journey through the days as a united pair,

Side by side, discussing tomorrow's open air.

Conversing about the sun and the ocean's gentle waves,

Sharing pain, nurturing hopes in the love that saves.

Together, we savor the fragrant scent of roses in bloom,

Watching raindrops on the window, our cozy room.

By the cool fire, we find tranquility's embrace,

Listening to melodies unknown, hearts in the same place.

We become a part of time, entwined in life's gentle stream,

In each other's company, we're free from agony, it seems.

Embracing peace, believing in love's graceful theme,

Together, we discover the beauty in life's radiant dream.

1990

IF

I f love courses through your veins, still alive and warm,

If my image remains framed within your heart, a cherished form,

If memories of those dark, empty nights endure,

If you've not denied your inner yearning, I'm sure.

If you honor the depth of your true feelings, so sincere,

Then let me be the path you choose to walk, my dear.

A breath of oxygen for you to always keep,

Words tattooed in the corner of your heart, love's secrets deep.

Let me be the dust of love that gently falls upon your face,

Until you trust my love's embrace, finding your place.

A fresh beginning as our old life calls,

If you still believe in our love's sacred halls.

If you gaze into the distant morn, seeking fate's sign,

Staring at the cracked door of our shared design,

Grant me forgiveness with grace reborn,

For in our love, it's never too late, my love, it's dawn.

1990

IN PURSUIT OF TOMORROW

With hope for grace in tomorrow's light,

I'll ignite my life, banish the darkest night.

Each day, though the path feels unbearably steep,

I'll march forward, sorrow to defeat, dreams to keep.

Kissing the dead trunk, I feel alive, spring's revival,

As years pass by, I await a new arrival,

The end of isolation's web, battles hard-fought and won,

Defeating death's spider, the strife is finally undone.

Blossoms emerge in life's flowing river,

Love the name we bestow, in hopes that hearts will quiver.

Perhaps a symbol, a story to borrow,

For novels and legends, a future yet untold to follow,

A bright tomorrow where love and passion unfold,

In the warmth of the sun, in the stories of old.

1990

EXILE'S EMBRACE

In this land of exile, a nation once proud and free,

Now captured, displaced, a shadow of what used to be.

Our thoughts adrift in mist, our cities left behind, we roam,

For some, it's love displaced, a precious tie unwoven from home.

In pain, we stand, with eyes that shed untold tears,

Bearing the weight of shared suffering, throughout the years.

Far from our homes, we endure the strife alone,

Separated from each other, in this world unknown.

Familiarity has faded as we drift apart,

Relationships and love, lost to the smothering heart.

In this exile, kindness and compassion are scarce,

In a world without nationality, we seek a familiar face.

A DIALOGUE WITH SORROW

My heart insists on a mood of weeping,

Longing to mourn, both day and night, in its keeping.

I implore it to look upon the world so wide,

Where suffering, pain, and sorrow coincide.

I say, "My dearest heart, please understand,

Life can't be embraced with sadness alone, and,

Tears in hand, let's not forget the joy that's real."

It answers, "If pain's left unhealed, a perpetual hell we feel.

FREE AND LIBERATED

I beseech you, spare me your bustling cities and endless nights,

I yearn not for faceless crowds and their dim lights.

Leave me in solitude where pure nights reside,

Alone in my world, in peaceful strides.

Let me linger with sweet memories of the past,

A liberated woman, free at last.

Why treat me as labor, selling me to another master?

I may be lonely, a little broken, but I'm not a disaster.

I possess love and unspoken words, unheard,

I won't be your kindred spirit, my spirit unblurred.

I am not a commodity in your bustling city's fray,

I am myself, strong, liberated, and defined my own way.

1989

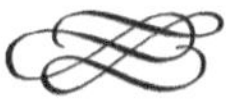

THE STONE HEART

Oh, all you lovers, listen to this truth I share,

To truly know, to be aware, if you dare.

His heart, a stone among stones, it dwells,

My weeks of tears, like a stream, his heart repels.

The dust of hatred remains, unyielding to my plea,

Even if I apologize with the world's sincerity.

In vain, I cry, scream, and groan for his forgiveness,

Yet, the silence of his heart, a stark emptiness.

Yes, oh lovers, grasp this truth, understand,

His heart, the hardest, like unyielding land.

Even if I offer a world of roses with a trembling hand,

His stone heart won't accept, won't understand.

Even if I become love's burning sun, so bright,

His sea of anger and resentment won't take flight.

Even if I become a fierce, destructive storm in the night,

His heart's cloud of bitterness won't yield its might.

Even if crows bear news of my final breath, he won't cry,

But a mystery hides in his eyes, as the days go by.

He took me in gently like a stream on a rock's hard crest,

But one day, his pride may bring him unrest.

Shattering his heart, breaking it underground's embrace,

And then, it will be me, the weeping cloud, I'll face.

Tears on his grave, like rain to the soil, I'll give,

A rose's root, his beauty in the grave, where he'll live.

A cricket chirping in the dark, cold night's embrace,

Whispering love's tales, in that sacred, silent place.

I'll build my love's house upon his tranquil grave,

Kiss his earth with memories, his eternal peace to save.

Breathing the cemetery's air, a soothing sense of release,

Hoping my love's warmth revives his cold, resting lease.

1989

SOLITUDE

Don't speak to me, just depart, I pray,
Leave me in solitude, let me find my way.
Allow me to burn with sorrow's unforgiving flame,
Transform into pain, a shadow without a name.
Let my desires turn to ashes in this fiery haze,
Go away, refrain from words in this complex maze.
Let me be, let me be alone in this vast zone,
With my misery, tears, and my mournful moan.
With a heart shattered and a wounded soul,
Go away, go away, let me reach my goal.
In the silence of my heart, let me reside,
In its sanctuary, let me heal, no longer hide.

1989

CALLING YOU

Summon all my dreams, hopes, and past regrets,

With what words, what message, what voice, no secrets.

To reach for you, to yearn and touch your heart's sweet art,

Seek your eyes, long for your embrace from the very start.

With love, I adore you, with regrets, I reminisce and rue,

I await your return, our moments together, long overdue.

Hoping for another day with you, our love forever in view.

In this Journey of the heart, my love remains true.

1989

ALONE

The door, seal the windows tight,
Draw the curtain, let in no light.

Send the world away, let them be gone,

I seek solitude, to reflect upon.

With my pain, my cries, and shadows blend,

Eyes filled with tears, let solitude descend.

Unplug the phones, silence all voices outside,

I crave solitude, where confessions reside.

Alone with my agony, my inner strife,

In silent moments, pondering the journey of life.

I want to be alone, if just for a while,

To find solace, within, reconcile.

1989

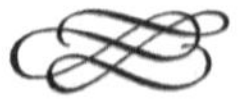

YEARNING

My broken heart cries out for your loving grace,

My lifeless gaze aches for your dreamy eyes from the start.

My bent existence moans, yearning for your embrace so tight,

My frozen hands tremble, seeking your warm guiding light.

1989

BURNED AND CRUMBLED

Burned and crumbled in life's aimless maze,
Broken from the ruins of my heart's disarray,
I've moaned and cried, lost in love's endless chase,
Yearned with tearful eyes, hope led astray.
Melted by the fire of love's relentless flame,
Separated, left with no other path to claim.

1988

HEART'S IMPRISONMENT

My heart, condemned to an eternal pain,

In sorrow's chains, it must remain.

Entwined with the burning agony's might,

Enduring the coldness of endless night.

The prison cage envelops my shattered soul's woe,

Incarcerated by the silent days where shadows grow.

This prison, now my solemn retreat,

A broken abode, filled with misery's drumbeat.

1988

SILENT HEART, REBELLIOUS EXISTENCE

In silence, my heart, my existence rebels,

Numbed by the stillness of nonexistence's spells.

My soul, in mourning, grieves my heart's demise,

Thoughts in shock at the painful goodbyes.

Isolation, the realm my heart inhabits in strife,

Living not as you live, defines my life.

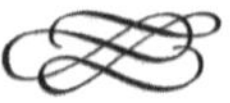

SORROWFUL REFLECTION

Oh, my eyes, transform into a sea on my sorrowed face,

Oh, my tears, cascade from the depths of my lamentation's grace,

Oh, mourning, sigh over the fiery flame of my heart's embrace.

1988

THE FLAMES OF SORROW

O burning flame of sorrow, scorching all in your wake,

Except for pain, you kindle, a ceaseless ache.

O moans that may seem in vain, a lament never spent,

Except for regret, you resonate, with torment unrelenting.

Within the heart's ruins, oppression finds its abode,

An owl of darkness, where shadows fearlessly rove

O eyes, transform into a sea on my veiled face,

Let tears wash away my soul's somber embrace.

From my gaze, let the tears flow, a river softly moaning,

And my sighs be the whispers of the flame, steadily glowing.

1988

MY AUTUMN

Oh, my autumn, how swiftly you've arrived,

Leaving me fragile, lifeless, and deprived.

Desires and dreams now laid to rest,

Like a single dry leaf, clinging, doing its best.

I'm lifeless, a gentle breeze could decree,

To stamp the death certificate, set me free.

My sky, a dark gray canvas of tears,

My night, a void, devoid of stars and fears.

Oh, my autumn, agent of change,

Arriving swiftly, my life you rearrange.

You touched the spirit of a once-magnificent core,

A woman of passion, hope, and dreams galore.

Crushing desires, silencing dreams it seems,

Oh, my autumn, a fleeting passage of dreams.

1988

DAMN

Why did you contend against us with such might?
With battle-hardened hands, delivering relentless spite.
For the deepest moans within my very soul, you mend,
My heart aches again, like a river's endless, groaning bend.
Burning sensations hold my life in chains, I know,
Woe to you, woe to life's unyielding ebb and flow.
Enduring disgrace and pain, nowhere to hide,
Our dreams now shattered, like fragile glass, they slide.
I've perished from the pain, cried with a heavy sigh,
Damn, why did you clash with us, oh endless strife
Our battles continue, this enduring dance of life.

1988

CHAINS OF SORROW

What should I do? In this obsidian snare,

No exit in sight, ensnared by deep despair.

Life's threads, a web I can't untangle or sever,

I beseech you to break these chains forever.

My pain unrelenting, my grief unrestrained,

In making my own trap strained, I've remained.

The oppressor of my tender heart, my frail frame,

Imprisons me in fear, my last breath but a flame.

I've tightened the shackles, a self-imposed fate,

Hoping to free my soul from this dire state.

In this prison of dread, where agony unfurls,

I yearn for salvation from life's cruel whirl.

1988

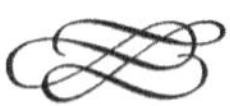

MY HEART'S LONELY LAMENT

In this lonely corner, my heart meets its end,

Surrounded by all, yet alone, in life's cage I descend.

A heart, bereft of beats, sighs in woeful woe,

Like a lonely autumn tree in the restless world's throes.

In humiliation, my heart takes its final bow,

Fragile and silent, with no sweetheart to vow.

Among shattered souls, it's frail and sere,

In an agonizing howl, my heart sheds its last tear.

In this loveless house, it quietly abides,

Beyond devotion's grasp, where it slowly hides.

In silence, my heart, existence in disarray,

Seeking a different path, yearning to convey.

My heart aches for my solitary existence,

My soul weeps for the heart's lost resonance.

Thoughts cry out in relentless refrain,

Why does the heart bear such a burden of pain?

The alchemist of love holds no cure for my heart,

To free myself from this life, I must depart.

1988

WINE WORSHIPER

L et's drink, let's inebriate our very souls,
Unveil our true selves and escape life's tolls.

Expand our perception like an endless sea,

Proclaim love and lovers, let our spirits roam free.

In this vessel, I reside, not in another's cup,

Within the cup of existence, I glimpse myself and look up.

While drowning within, I seek the innermost core,

Witnessing the heart's tears and sadness galore.

The shadow of my heart sits by the cold fire, in despair,

A sea of sight, born from anger and tears, laid bare.

From the garden of my sweet love, tulips rise and wither,

Hopes from my enduring love, they, too, did slither.

In the continuing tale of sorrow and woe,

I spoke to my heart, my fragile heart, in tow,

"Let us declare life absurd, in the world of existence's spree,

Let's deem it as nothingness, and let deception flee.

For demons and jackals disguise their deceit,

Let's bury this wicked love, with hatred's stone completely.

In the days of drunkenness, life we shall deny,

In the world of existence, absurdity shall lie."

Let's be intoxicated every day, in days of old,

Embrace life's madness, as its tales are told.

With its lies, its arrogance, its empty promise,

We'll call it nothingness, life's grand premise.

1988

IN SEARCH OF SOLACE

Where are you going, to another sorrow's door?
Why embrace the pain of oppression, evermore?
My heart, where are you headed, my dear?
Why hide your sighs and passions, I fear?
Soul, where do you pause in sin's shadowed den?
World, where do you turn from my solitude, then?
In search of solace, where is your gaze so deep?
Why block all other pathways, secrets to keep?

1988

DESIRE TO EMBRACE LIFE'S ESSENCE

I yearn to be a candle in the darkest nights,

Burning with pain and suffering, igniting shared lights.

A flower in the garden of Broken Hearts, I'd bloom,

A weeping cloud in the sky's vast, endless room.

I long to become a raging ocean wave with grace,

The dawn and morning breeze's gentle embrace.

A star marking the passage of time so bright,

Tears, waiting to fall in the quiet of night.

I aspire to be a passionate fire, love's charm,

Shouting from the depths, a cry with no harm.

To suffer in solitude, and in sadness weep,

Becoming the Truth, untold secrets to keep.

A love bird, in the night, my love unfolds,

Singing sweet songs, our story retold.

1987

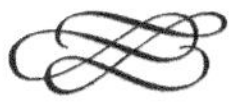

POET REFLECTIONS

Poetry, the furnace where inner sorrows find their place,

Love, the path through life I walk, embracing grace,

Life, the burden of sins I carry with care,

And death, the ultimate freedom from this earthly wear.

1987

LAMENT OF A BROKEN HEART

Why have you sown sorrow within my heart's chamber,

Igniting my feeble cries, feeding your own pain's ember?

Oh, my heart, once warm, now cold and burning in grief,

My lips, once smiling, now sealed in mournful relief.

My once vivid eyes now dim and heavy with tears,

A drunken gaze stumbles through a landscape of fears.

Why did you cast upon me the spell of nonexistence,

Affixing a seal of sorrow to my love's fragile existence?

My days grow darker, each one a cell of despair,

Nights become prisons of sorrow, the heart laid bare.

The once colorful sky now a blank canvas, stark,

The sun of my life extinguished, leaving a shadowy mark.

Why, my Lord, have you rained spears of sadness upon me?

Why did you bestow your loveless heart's decree?

Why tear me apart, drop by drop, without relent?

Why not bury me bit by bit, to ease this torment,

Why unravel my moments, my life in this descent?

1987

A CRY OF SELF-DISPOSSESSION

O friend, behold my utter destitution,

In disdain, my world I loathe with bitter resolution.

Gaze upon these lifeless eyes I bear,

Peering within, pain they cause, a heavy burden to wear.

O friend, take heed of my restless, pounding heart,

A relentless beat from which I wish to depart.

O, friend, see how my sanity, I've nearly forsaken,

As I drift further from my own self, feeling overtaken.

Amidst the torrents of unceasing tears,

I endure the cruel weight of persecution's fears,

And crumble beneath time's relentless sway,

Questioning the purpose of my frenzied way.

O friend, perceive, I'm but invisible dust,

A drifting presence, life's meaning turned unjust.

O friend, acknowledge, in the drifting dust I roam,

A stranger even to myself, in desolation's home.

1987

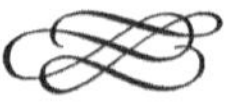

UNYIELDING TIDES OF THE HEART

My heart soars upon the wings of the wind,

Effortlessly adrift on endless waves,

In search of its very essence, its core within.

Within this heart, no escape, no peace, it seems,

Raw emotions surge through these coursing veins,

Unsilenced, untamed, like endless streams.

On this unending journey, rest remains distant,

Misery unfolds, relentless, day and night,

No clear distinction between light and dark, persistent.

Within me, no desires, no thoughts to seek,

The era's secrets, concealed and unrevealed,

As I navigate this existence, bold yet meek.

1987

INK OF THE UNKNOWN

I write, though my purpose remains unclear,

Words flow seeking a muse unknown,

Compelled by an unseen force that's near.

The pen, my loyal servant, obeys my command,

It conveys the unspoken depths I feel,

As waves kiss the shore, making their stand.

Why do I write, for whom, I cannot tell,

The muse remains silent, shrouded in mist,

In nature's tears and ancient questions, I dwell.

The wheels of time turn, leaving their mark,

Embraced by the vastness of space, the past,

In search of meaning, for whom, for what, I find.

1987

WHISPERS OF THE DEPARTED SOUL

I know not what has become of me,

I journeyed to the farthest horizons, now intertwined with the earth.

My heart weeps in separation's torment,

Eyes filled with life's anguish.

Come, my friend, reach out your hand,

For it is virtuous to aid the feeble.

Why, oh why,

Can I not cry from the depths of my heart,

To confide in God my hidden secrets?

That I may not be reduced to mere wax, like a candle,

That I may not be consumed like a blazing fire, turned to ashes.

Oh, merciful Lord, I have a humble plea,

I despise dwelling in anguish while life brightens its path.

Why, then, do you appear vengeful?

154

What wrongs have you seen in me that my heart weeps like a river,

And my essence is surrendered to the cold abyss?

My heart is engulfed by mighty waves,

My body merges with the earth in swirling sands.

Why, O Lord, have you done this?

You have entombed me with my despairing cries.

If I were God, I would not inflict such cruelty.

If distinctions exist in this realm,

Why are they not evident?

If I have wronged you, you have wronged me as well,

So what sets me apart from you, my Lord?

If there is a secret, share it with me,

I promise to bury it within the soil, along with my own form.

So that one day, perhaps, blossoms may emerge,

Revealing what was concealed and veiled,

And may the whispers of this secret echo among the flowers, nothing more.

1982

AWAKENING OF THE SOUL

Awaken, O memories, memories of my existence,
Memories of how I fell in love.

O herald, proclaim with fervor,

I am no longer the solitary maiden, nor the crowded city,

I have become a duality,

Two beings, two hearts, two minds, two breaths.

O tears of joy, flow and grace my cheeks,

No longer the weeping, sorrowful eyes of yore,

I shed no tears of anguish,

For now, tears of happiness accompany me, the joy of rebirth.

O eyes, peer into mine, delve deep,

No longer the eyes of despair,

But the romantic stars that fixate on their beloveds.

Dandelions, don your white attire,

Dance and carry my message to the world,

That I have been born anew,

Streams, gush, and roll,

No more the arid and rugged terrain,

No longer the wounded thorn.

O gentle winds, come hither,

Dissipate the somber clouds from my heart,

The sun of my heart has ascended.

O hearts, beat, my heart is thawed and lively,

Fresh blood courses through, rejuvenating my essence.

O life, embrace, extend your arms,

My spirit is no longer frozen,

The nights of longing are behind me.

Summon the stars to amplify your radiance,

Bid the moon to observe me,

As a sweet smile graces my lips, accompanied by laughter.

O artists, O painters,

Render and illustrate my visage,

To hang upon the city's gate,

So people may see, it is no longer just me, but an existence imbued
with purpose.

Writers, pen my story,

Let it become a tome for all to read,

And comprehend that it is no longer just me, but a resplendent
soul.

O lovers, behold and understand,

I am the magnificence of love among lovers.

1982

SACRIFICE FOR LOVE

I transform into dew, gracing your cheeks like spring petals,

As torrential rain, nurturing love's seeds in your heart's arid soil.

Then, an ardent sun, igniting you with my fervent essence,

As a root, conquering your very core,

Becoming the path you tread, a breeze whisking weariness from your face.

I'm your constant shadow, accompanying every moment,

The fine dust of love upon your countenance, seeking entry to the city of lovers.

A flower positioned on your path, for you to plant within your heart's gateway.

I persist for you to encounter and believe,

Belief to unearth reality, and reality to hold the truth.

I'll be scripted, for you to inscribe within your heart's small notebook,

Transforming into artwork, a masterpiece in your heart's gallery.

An ardent love, for you to fall for, and a lover for you to reciprocate.

Evolving into a memory, etched deep within your thoughts,

A wooden reed serenading with love's melodies.

Morning breeze caresses your weary spirit,

Hope for your desires, a desire for your convictions.

I transform into a tranquil sea, inviting you to dive into my depths,

A pristine azure sky offering the purity of my existence for your flight.

A guiding star, harbinger of your nightly desires,

Evolving into a puzzle, waiting for you to decipher.

Your canvas, inviting you to craft a masterpiece,

A masterpiece awaiting your transformation into an epic.

A graceful white dove, entrapped within your heart's golden cage,

A dainty dandelion, donning a white gown, harbinger of joy among lovers.

I persist in beauty until you gaze upon me and embrace my verity,

Your secret receptacle, harboring your secrets in the recesses of my heart.

I become your night raven, clucking only the truth of my existence,

A lovebird, serenading you solely with love's melodies during the night.

The very particles of air for you to breathe me in,

A garment you don, taking shape upon your form.

I'm a synopsis of your life, destined to end our story.

DECLARATIONS OF LOVE

I declare my love with the rhythmic beating of my heart,

Enslaved by your golden heart's allure.

I proclaim my love through thoughts,

As my heart's roots sprout from the seeds of your affection.

My gaze stands as a constant sentinel, ever awaiting your return,

Whispering, 'I love you.'

Within the labyrinthine recesses of your mind, I etch these words:

With a pen now devoid of ink,

And paper no longer left to be inked.

Yet still, I profess my love with faint script in a paper's corner,

With weathered hands upon the scorching beach's sand.

Upon the forest wood, I inscribe 'I love you,'

With the warmth of my embrace, a gracious host to your presence.

I declare with the fervor of my heart, 'I love you,'

Upon the crimson petals of a flower arranged for you, the words 'I love you' are gracefully written.

1981

IN QUEST OF LOVE'S ANSWERS

Which river might cleanse the swamps of rotting thoughts?

Which cedar will stand amidst the verdant plains of my dreams?

Which mountain dares to withstand life's radiant splendor?

Which storyteller harmonizes their tale with mine?

Which freedom-dove can soar through this masked realm's poisoned air?

Which steadfast light can pierce my obsidian heart's shroud?

What tears shall flow from a love-stricken eye?

Which innocent love butterfly hovers around the artificial glow of vain people?

Which affectionate dandelion shall convey my love's message?

Which bloom may grace my soulless vessel?

Which raindrops may quench the parched atmosphere of my existence?

What torment and sighs may escape my being?

For I am in love, with lips parched for love, pain, and sighs.

1981

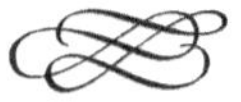

WHO AM I?

From which descent, what heritage, from which nation?

From what vantage point, does the outcry come – fury, venom, hate?

From which class, from which city – a city where people wear masks of opulence and hide their true identities?

Who am I?

From which love, tenderness, friendship, sacrifices, and faiths do I originate?

Am I born of wolves, lions, or jackals? Of destitution, oppression, misery, or fortune?

Who am I?

A creature that breathes, walks, eats, and sleeps?

Or one that lives with unbridled freedom?

Who am I?

An ardent lover chasing the artificial candle of life's glow?

Or a hopeful soul seeking the light of possibility?

165

Who am I?

A freedom dove singing the song of liberty?

Or a captive dove confined within the gilded bars of materialism?

Who am I?

A rhythm of life, in tune with the sunrise and sunset?

Or a phantom sun, rising and setting like a sleepwalker?

Who am I?

A thought to be suggested, a proposition to be a theory?

A theory that becomes a law, a law that liberates.

Who am I?

A method to be experienced, an experience to be understood, learned, and realized?

Or a genuine belief, the truth that is a fact.

Who am I?

A pen in the hands of an executioner, boasting of lions and jackals?

Or an expression of sorrow, the key to addressing deprivation?

Who am I?

A fixed gaze upon the shadows of lions and jackals' paths?

Or a vision of solutions on the endless dark roads?

Who am I?

A heartbeat resonating with every pulse of life?

Steadfast steps along the path of love.

Who am I?

A warm, eager embrace welcoming the existence of deprived children?

Or a frozen hug for the soulless?

Who am I?

Feeble, trembling hands, hesitant to hold an orphan's hand?

A legacy of pure self-sacrifice or a heritage mired in the swamp of corruption?

Who am I?

A cry of anger, rage, hatred, revenge, resentment, pain, and oppression?

A storm of fury shattering the soulless existence of jackals?

Or a tempest caressing the homes of the deprived?

Who am I?

A smile on the lips of innocent children?

Or a grin on the lips of cunning foxes?

Who am I?

A joyful breeze softly caressing the colorless face of an orphaned girl?

Or a chilly gust upon the joyless countenance of a sad girl?

Who am I?

An account of the deprivations of time?

Or the fragmented image of future happiness?

Who am I?

A period of epochs, a period of history, history of lives?

The foamy sea of fantasies or a boundless sea of movements?

Who am I?

A leap forward, the movement of movements,

The motion of the inhabitants, a dwelling of fears, fear of ignorance.

Who am I?

A summary of collections or a collection of categories,

A handful of groups, a group of multitudes,

A multitude of singulars, a singular among individuals,

A person within the community, and perhaps a summation of the summations.

Who am I?

Why so, and for what reason?

Why this, as it should be?

Who am I?

A stone hardening the hearts of the oppressors,

A cypress, a symbol of stability.

Who am I?

A chain around the necks of captives,

Or a chain around hatred, vengeance, rage, and revenge, tightening until the revolution erupts.

And in short, who am I?

What am I seeking?

How do I navigate life?

What is my purpose?

Where am I heading? Who am I?

1980

O HUMAN

Love seeks its beloved,

Envy covets that which is desired,

Revenge hungers for the bitterness of hatred's taste,

Rain quenches the arid lands' thirst,

The sun warms destitute hearts with its radiant embrace.

Water yearns to merge in the river's gentle embrace,

The river, in its turn, craves the vastness of the sea's wide expanse,

The sea, in its yearning, seeks the boundless ocean's touch.

The romantic butterfly flits toward the candle's flame,

The candle, ablaze with ardent passion,

Yearns for the essence of love.

The bee, forever eager, seeks spring's fragrant blooms,

Life itself longs for the experience of being,

Time turns to trace the heavens' rotation,

And space, embracing the destiny of all existence.

Thoughts, ready to make sacrifices,

Hearts, open to love and kindness,

Eyes, in pursuit of beauty, radiance, and purity,

Hands, reaching out with compassion,

Feet, walking boundless paths and unending goals.

Each breath an inhale and an ascent in the lover's presence,

The pen, ardently yearning for the paper's caress,

The paper, eager for the ink's inscription.

In essence, all creatures are seekers and lovers,

But you, O human, what are your desires and yearnings?

Whom do you cherish? What is it that you pursue?

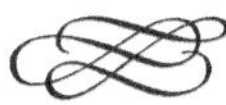

NOTHING TRANSFORMED INTO YES

There was no dandelion to convey a message of hope,

Till a smile graced his frozen lips,

Not the gentle breeze to embrace and caress her weary soul,

No fervent plea to lovingly call her name,

To cry out her name and whisper, "My sweet child, my cherished one,"

With loving arms to cradle her.

No gentle hand to wipe tears from her precious pearls,

In the frigid winter's embrace, shielding her pallid cheeks,

No willing lips to kiss her colorless ones,

Not a melody to sing a lullaby.

No comforting hug to enfold her,

To alleviate her suffering and disperse the dust of sorrow from her face,

No compassionate heart to take pity,

No butterfly to alight on her golden hair,

To pirouette and raise her spirits to joy.

No moment of anticipation to await her,

No glimmer of hope to mend her shattered heart,

No heavenly savior to rescue her fragile being,

No flower to bloom, no flower to scent and pluck.

No burning love to cherish her without departing,

No storyteller to recount her anguished tale,

No pen, no paper to inscribe her life,

No author to depict her existence with its bitter memories.

No witness to these injustices of life,

No memory preserved to be etched in the somber annals of existence.

How she passed away alone, reduced to a speck of insignificant dust,

No eyes wept for her excruciating demise, no heartfelt her pain.

No, indeed, no, nothing transformed into yes,

No cries against this cruelty and injustice,

No anger ignited to stir a movement,

Not the kind that brings forth life,

No iron fists raised in passionate protest,

Shouting with all their might.

No bullet aimed at the unfeeling heart of life,

No marching steps to stand against these injustices,

No awakened conscience to defy the harsh world,

No thoughts that transformed into action.

There was no storm to sweep away the dust of this cruelty from the world's existence,

Yes, my friend,

There was no; nothing transformed into yes.

1979

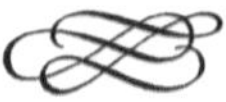

THE ALLURE OF DARKNESS

I cherish the night, for it washes away the mundane,

As darkness falls, my thoughts grow profound.

The night whispers, urging me to seek solace,

To ponder, reflect, and ask for guidance.

In its quiet, I sense the struggles of the unseen,

Dwelling in shadows, buried in their dark abyss.

I relish the night, for I'm suspended in-between,

Not on my land, fraught with hatred and spite.

Nor in the heavens, heavy with the oppressed's sighs,

But in the night, where I find my respite.

The darkness liberates me from the day's monotony,

In its embrace, I connect with another realm, another reality.

THE MANY FACES OF LOVE

Love takes the form of a delicate dandelion's dance,

Breathing life into every lover's sweet romance.

It blooms like a flower, sought by hearts that yearn,

A bud waiting to unfurl, in love's embrace, we learn.

Love surges like the wild sea's uncontrollable waves,

Cleansing, purifying, in its depths, our love engraves.

It's a rain cloud, washing away all that's unclean,

A gentle breeze, caressing lovers' hair, yet unseen.

A running river, laid in the path of every lover's quest,

A force of nature, guiding hearts to find their best.

Yet, at times, love takes a different face, my friend,

Like a scarecrow, sowing fear, causing love to bend.

A shadow of a cloud, shrouding hearts in darkness and despair,

Sometimes love roars like thunder, catching us unaware.

And, yes, my friend, love may appear in false pearls' guise,

Chaining the lover's heart, in captive love's disguise.

1979

A HOPEFUL WORLD

When I am alive, no more shall the cries of impoverished children ring,

When I live, I long to stand among my fellow human beings.

With life, cruelty and divisions shall dissolve away,

No pain, no sadness, just a brighter, unified day.

Hope will dance in the eyes of innocent orphaned souls,

In a world free from hatred and anger, we'll set our goals.

When I am alive, no more wars or oppression shall ensnare,

Dreaming of a clean, beautiful society, beyond compare.

1978

LIFE'S ESSENCE

Life is love, a cherished gift to embrace,
A belief, a journey we must faithfully trace.
It's an inner cry, waiting to be shouted loud and clear,
A path, a goal, a course we'll persevere.
Life offers both bitter and sweet moments, beliefs to uphold,
A living history, through eras and times untold.
A radiant sun that warms frozen souls, it's agreed,
Life, a love that must be cherished indeed.

THE ETERNAL TRAVELER

A traveler in search of life's endless mystery,
Sibling of the wind, born from the waves' history.

Unceasing legs, a mind that never rests,

Chasing life's elusive trail, on an eternal quest.

Guided by the white bird of freedom's flight,

Leaving behind new paths in the fading light.

This poet, a constant traveler, never still,

Always hoping for tomorrow, chasing time's thrill.

In the reeds of the wood, life met with death's breath,

Proclaiming, "From sunrise to sunset, until my final breath."

Our immortal traveler, whose quest never ceased,

In silence, found no life, forever at peace.

A traveler in spirit and mind, the journey endures,

No room for despair, as hope's fire still assures.

Leaving a backpack, a gift to remember and keep,

A reminder of the journey, in eternal sleep.

A TRIBUTE TO KHOSROW GOLSARAKHI

I write from the depths of my heart,

The poetry of freedom, a heroic art,

A tribute to Golsarakhi's sacrifice and might,

Poetry for freedom and its radiant light.

Where is that vibrant blush so grand?

Tell me, who thinks as I, who understands?

Speak of his name, his enduring legacy,

His words, our words, shared by all of humanity.

His presence within the prison, a dreadful plight,

Yet he stood strong as a mountain, his might,

His name, a guerrilla who paid life's ultimate cost,

Khosrow Golsarakhi, in freedom's name embossed.

Yes, I write from the depth of my soul,

A poem for the thunder, the one who took his toll,

A rose whose name embodies compassion and free thought,

A guerrilla who fearlessly fought against tyranny's plot.

He battled the wind, high and valiant,

Roaring fiercely, evil trembled, compliant,

His bright eyes pierced the darkness and despair,

Expressing his hatred, a burden he couldn't bear.

Death was to him an enigma, unclear,

A word meant to incite fear and steer,

But he, unafraid, faced all with might,

For his people, he sacrificed, fought for their rights.

A people once muted, unable to sing,

Now rise to dismantle corruption, to bring,

To life his words, ideals, principles so true,

For they now see him as an eternal, enduring view.

Long live his name, long live his soul,

Though he can't witness his people's goal,

Their striving for a brighter future's grace,

In your empty place, my hero, we embrace.

1978

THE WINE OF FREEDOM

O sister, brother, father, mother,

And you, self-sacrificing human being,

I address you, solely you,

Drink, drink,

From this wine, the wine that only lived in your dreams,

Drink, drink,

From the wine that seemed a mirage, a distant, untouchable scheme,

Drink, drink,

From this unending wine, the wine of freedom,

Freedom achieved through the blood of heroes,

Freedom that should be honored for the generations to come.

So, partake of this elixir of life,

The wine of freedom for hearts, minds, souls, and bodies in years yet to thrive.

1978

ECHOES OF SUFFERING

I am filled with the sorrow of injustice,

With poverty and a lack of human compassion.

Burn the walls of my heart for the pain of the poor.

I mourn day and night, overwhelmed by the suffering of the sick.

I speak of the world's unfaithfulness,

I write of the divisions among human beings.

I am brimming with this sadness,

Witnessing humanity's agony.

I do not know where true love resides,

Is there a world free from pain?

Is there a place untouched by sorrow?

I know that within this dream, I will smolder,

Vanished, buried in an elusive reverie dream.

A brush within my mind paints only the sorrow of humanity,

A sorrow that rises in a blaze.

1976

TEARS FROM THE SKY

R ain fell upon me, drop by drop,

On the roof of the house, it pattered,

Seeming as though the sky itself wailed in anguish,

Playing a mournful, haunting melody.

The sky wept, tears of sorrow cascading,

I watched each tear descend, dot by dot,

Transforming the world into a watery expanse,

A ceaseless, relentless cry.

I pondered the source of this affliction,

Why the world must be drenched in pain and heaven's sorrow,

Why, indeed?

1974

ODE TO SPRING

O, Spring, your beauty rivals a vibrant bouquet of flowers,

You're like a heavenly temple in our earthly hours.

Your existence is a realm of love and purity, it's true,

You are the season that adorns every imperfection we view.

You beautify the naked face of nature with your gentle touch,

O, Spring, you're a symbol of beauty and grace that means so much.

We bless you, dear Spring, for all that you bestow,

For you are freedom and beauty, in full bloom, you glow.

1974

IN PRAISE OF NATURE

What is it that eludes my description?

I seek assistance to articulate its essence.

What is it that our conversations and debates cannot truly justify, its magnificent being?

What is it that renders the pen powerless, unable to capture its entirety?

What bestows joy and happiness upon an individual?

Do you know the pen? Do you know the paper?

It is Nature, Nature, possessing a name of beauty and a heart of purity.

It is Nature that has enchanted me.

It is that Nature which has permeated my soul.

Nature, in which everything and everyone finds unity,

The intricate dance of life, with moments of both sorrow and joy.

All is the handiwork of Nature.

Yes, Nature, our resplendent Nature, stands proudly tall.

1974

CUNNING SNAKE

O musician, your melody flows so well,

But I beg you, heed those tender hands and the mouth that does tell.

For the wily snake, harbinger of enmity and vice,

Plays games, O musician, heed this advice.

Play on, let the serpent slither on its way,

Engage in its schemes, its treachery, have your say.

Play, O musician, yet don't ignore the avian cries,

Shrieking in fear, afraid of the snake's cunning guise.

O virtuous musician, why do you play this tune?

I can bear it no more, as the serpents make my heart swoon.

I don't wish to witness the deeds of these deceivers,

Their trickery and venom, as they prey on the believers.

I don't wish to see the biting poison they unleash,

Their hissing, the suffering of birds within their reach.

Those poor birds, they cry and scream in despair,

"Be gone, striped snake, with your venomous snare!"

The treacherous snake, the cunning snake so sly,

Always proclaiming, "It's my turn, it's my sky, birds shall die!"

I yearn to see them pay for their wicked art,

To sacrifice them to nature's justice, a fitting part.

When will my year of peace and harmony arrive?

When will the birds rejoice, fully alive?

May my prophecy come true, the birds content and plump,

When hatred and conflict finally take a slump?

* 9 7 8 9 6 5 5 7 8 6 5 7 6 *